Cold Salmon

A Play

John Bowen

A SAMUEL FRENCH ACTING EDITION

FOUNDED 1830

SAMUELFRENCH-LONDON.CO.UK
SAMUELFRENCH.COM

Copyright © 1998 by John Bowen
All Rights Reserved

COLD SALMON is fully protected under the copyright laws of the British Commonwealth, including Canada, the United States of America, and all other countries of the Copyright Union. All rights, including professional and amateur stage productions, recitation, lecturing, public reading, motion picture, radio broadcasting, television and the rights of translation into foreign languages are strictly reserved.

ISBN 978-0-573-12032-9

www.samuelfrench-london.co.uk

www.samuelfrench.com

For Amateur Production Enquiries

United Kingdom and World excluding North America

plays@SamuelFrench-London.co.uk

020 7255 4302/01

Each title is subject to availability from Samuel French, depending upon country of performance.

CAUTION: Professional and amateur producers are hereby warned that COLD SALMON is subject to a licensing fee. Publication of this play does not imply availability for performance. Both amateurs and professionals considering a production are strongly advised to apply to the appropriate agent before starting rehearsals, advertising, or booking a theatre. A licensing fee must be paid whether the title is presented for charity or gain and whether or not admission is charged.

The professional rights in this play are controlled by Casarotto Ramsay Associates, Waverley House, 7-12 Noel Street, London, W1F 8GQ.

No one shall make any changes in this title for the purpose of production. No part of this book may be reproduced, stored in a retrieval system, or transmitted in any form, by any means, now known or yet to be invented, including mechanical, electronic, photocopying, recording, videotaping, or otherwise, without the prior written permission of the publisher. No one shall upload this title, or part of this title, to any social media websites.

The right of John Bowen to be identified as author of this work has been asserted by him in accordance with Section 77 of the Copyright, Designs and Patents Act 1988

CHARACTERS

Harry Farnham
Elsie
Angie Outhwaite
Beth Farnham
Liz
Janice
Pearson
Rosemary
Lester
Dad

The action of the play takes place in the neglected graveyard of a little church

Time: the present. A summer's day

CHARACTERS OF THE PLAY

Some of the characters are dead and some are living. The dead can see and hear the living, but are unable to communicate with them. The living cannot see or hear the dead and do not know that they are there.

The Dead

Harry Farnham, 64. Harry died in 1970 and has been waiting by his grave ever since for his wife to join him.

Elsie, 70s. Impossible to be sure when she died because her grave is unmarked. She waits by it in the vague hope that some member of her family will turn up to look for her some day.

Dad, 60s. He died earlier in the year and was cremated. His family has assembled to scatter his ashes at the tomb of his ancestors.

The Living

Angie Owthwaite, late 50s. Harry's daughter.

Beth Farnham, early 90s, although the actress playing her should be younger. Harry's wife, grown old and deaf and rather gaga; she has to be in a wheelchair for any outing. At the end of the play, Beth dies and is able—now looking much younger—to join her husband.

Liz, 30s. Daughter to Dad. A teacher. Unmarried.

Janice, early 40s. Sister-in-law to Liz. Socially mobile upwards, a great one for the finer things in life.

Pearson, early 40s. Brother to Liz, husband to Janice.

Rosemary, 14. Daughter to Pearson and Janice. Sulky, unhappy: her parents worry that she may become anorexic.

Lester, late 20s. Younger brother to Liz and Pearson. Gay but not in the least camp.

PRODUCTION NOTE

The church, although mentioned, is not seen. What is essential is that the church and graveyard are high on a cliff above the sea, probably somewhere on the Lancashire coast, but any company mounting the play is at liberty to site it on any other more local cliff and adjust the dialogue and dialect accordingly. The edge of the cliff is not far from the front of the stage: we do not need to bother with a fence or low wall which would only interfere with sight-lines.

Depending on the year when the play is performed, time references can be adjusted, as long as the year of Harry Farnham's death is about 28 years before the date of the performance.

The easiest way to make the humps in front of the gravestones might be to use Gro-bags covered with the plastic grass found in greengrocers' shops. The large grave would use three Gro-bags pushed together and one across them at the top; the small grave would need only one Gro-bag. The Gro-bag at the top of the large grave should have a (concealed) slit in it so that earth can be removed and an urn inserted.

COLD SALMON

A day in summer—late morning or early afternoon

A section of the neglected graveyard of a little church, now hardly used

We are concerned with two graves, one a rather grand family tomb, the other near it but a little farther downstage, smaller, with only one occupant. The family tomb has a large gravestone—large enough for us to be able to conceal one male actor, Dad, and one smallish female ASM behind it from the beginning of the play. The inscriptions on the slab—names and dates and such—have weathered and are no longer readable

The other gravestone is smaller, just a stone cross on a base. Here the inscription is recent enough for us to be able to read it...

> *Sacred To the Memory of*
> **HARRY FARNHAM**
> *1906-1970*
> *Gone But Not Forgotten*

...and it covers only half the space available on the headstone

Both stones have a sort of hump in front of them to mark the grave itself. On the hump in front of the small grave is a container with dead flowers in it. A third, unmarked, hump is DL

At the beginning of the play two people are on stage. Both are dead, waiting for the living. Harry, sixty-four years old, stands behind his gravestone. Elsie is in her seventies and sits propped against the end of the unmarked grassy hump, extreme DL. *They do not need any special make-up, but both should be dressed entirely in grey: grey cardigan, shirt, trousers, socks and shoes for Harry; shapeless grey dress, stockings and shoes for Elsie*

Elsie I sit here. The years go by, but nobody comes.
Harry How could they? Unmarked grave: you could be anywhere. They should have stumped up for a plaque.
Elsie They'd no money. Never had. She used to borrow from *me*, and I'ad nowt but me pension. Come round with a packet of Mint Imperials of a Wednesday and go through me purse before she went to Bingo. I could do with one of them Mint Imperials now. Something to suck, it's occupation. (*She pauses*) You'd think someone might look in.
Harry Your lot? They've moved most like. Sold up. Moonlight flit.
Elsie There was plenty of those.
Harry They could be passed on themselves by now. How long is it—forty year you've been here? *She* won't wait around. She'll be away up to the great Bingo Hall in the sky.
Elsie There was kids—two girls and a lad—my grandchildren. They might take it into their heads. I'll sit a bit longer.

Angie is heard from UL

Angie (*off*) Here we are, then, Mother!

Angie appears, pushing her mother, Beth, in a wheelchair, and comes down to Harry's grave. Angie is in her late fifties, Beth in her nineties (though the actress who plays her should be much younger). Beth is deaf and never says anything in answer to a question but "very nice". On her lap there is a plastic bag containing a pot of seasonal flowers. She is wearing a long coat, to cover up the grey clothes beneath, and a hat

Not a drop of rain, and as for the wind up here it's the merest

Cold Salmon

zephyr. We're very lucky; we should thank our lucky stars. (*She bends to shout, speaking distinctly as one does to the deaf, and moving her lips to be read*) It's turned out temperate, Mother. We should thank our stars.

Beth Very nice.

Angie Have you got the flowers? (*Loudly*) Flowers! (*She picks the plastic bag off Beth's lap and takes out the pot of flowers*) Lovely flowers for Dad. He always loved his flowers. (*During the following, she makes the swap, new flowers for dead, putting the dead flowers in the plastic bag*)

Elsie It's the lad I had hope for. Won half a crown at the age of seven singing *Land of Hope and Glory* in the Amateur Hour on Southport pier. She had it off him, of course, quicker than spitting, but I thought he might grow up to be famous and come back looking for me.

Harry It's not easy adjusting to a change of foliage every month.

Angie gives the plastic bag back to Beth

Angie Hold that.

There is the sound of a car stopping in the road outside the churchyard and a car door slams

Elsie Someone's coming.

Liz comes in from UL. She is in her thirties, a teacher at a school in Northampton. She has a shoulder-bag containing her contribution to a picnic over one shoulder, and carries a piece of card, consulting it for directions. She looks up and sees Angie and Beth

Liz Hullo...? I'm sorry to disturb you. I'm looking for a... (*She approaches a little way, consults the card*) It's a grave near the cliff. Name of... (*She decides that the larger grave is the one she's looking for*) This must be it. Bit tricky finding this place.

Angie gives her the half-nod, half-smile which is as far as she is prepared to go in conversation with a total stranger in a public place

Harry Aye, it is an' all. (*To Elsie*) Could this be one of yours maybe?
Elsie I wouldn't think so.

Liz looks at her wristwatch

Liz Nobody else arrived? I seem to be early. In fact, I know I'm late. So the world goes. (*She explains*) It's a family party. We're supposed to be joining up here.
Angie (*to Beth*) We'll just have a word with the Almighty inside the church now, Mother, and you can come out and sit with Dad for a bit afterwards. (*Loudly*) Going inside! To pray!
Beth Very nice.

Angie wheels Beth away UR. *Liz shrugs. Again there is the sound of a car stopping on the road. Angie turns her head and speaks to Liz while continuing on her way*

Angie This'll be your lot, I expect.

Angie exits with Beth, while four doors on the newly arrived car are heard closing

Liz Seems I've got the right day, then. (*She tries to make out the inscription on the gravestone*) "Until the day breaks and the shadows flee." I'll believe it when it happens.

Janice—in her early forties, upwardly mobile so that her natural northern accent has been overlaid by posh—arrives from UL, *stops, looks about her and sees Liz. She carries a large handbag*

Janice There you are, Liz! (*She turns and shouts over her shoulder*) She's here. You can bring the picnic. (*She comes down towards Liz*)

Cold Salmon

Liz I brought some sandwiches and a thermos of coffee. I hope that's all right.
Janice You're very kind, but you shouldn't have bothered. We have a sufficiency. (*She shouts* UL) Over here, Pearson.

Her husband, Liz's brother, Pearson, also in his forties, appears UL. *He is loaded with two cool-bags, a large car rug, two folding chairs and a small folding stool. He is followed by his daughter, Rosemary, fourteen, who carries nothing, and by Lester, in his twenties, the younger brother. Lester carries a plastic bag containing an urn wrapped in bubblewrap*

Elsie None of these.
Harry Well, of course not. The lady said they're a family party.
Elsie I give everybody the once-over just in case.
Janice Help your father with the picnic, Rosemary.

Rosemary looks at her father, deadpan, and holds out a hand

Pearson You can take the stool.

Rosemary takes the folding stool

Rosemary Where do you want it?
Pearson Anywhere.
Lester Why don't you give *me* something to carry? I've got nothing here.
Pearson There's really no need. It's no weight at all. Just a light collation.

He and Lester move on to join Janice and Liz. Rosemary stays where she is, holding the stool

Liz There were roadworks on the M6: I was afraid I'd be late.
Lester Meaning we're later? Well, it's my fault, I'm afraid.
Liz Don't be so prickly, Lester. There wasn't a subtext.

During the following dialogue, Janice relieves Pearson of his cargo bit by bit, opening the chairs and setting them down in front of the grave, laying out the rug in front of the chairs and the cool-bags on the rug

Janice We had to pick Lester up from the station at Preston. His car's off the road. It wasn't his fault. The train was late, as they usually are these days: I don't know how people manage.
Lester (*indicating the plastic bag*) Where do you want this?
Janice Just put it down by the gravestone, please.
Lester What is it?
Janice It's your father, so please treat it gently.
Lester (*alarmed*) You what?
Liz The ashes? Loose?
Pearson In a tasteful urn.
Liz I thought Mother had them.
Pearson She didn't want them—said they made her uncomfortable, like being watched all the time: she had enough of that while he was alive. So I've been looking after them.
Liz At your place?
Pearson Up to a point. Janice didn't like the idea either, so he's been in the boot of the car. Travelled all over the country these last few months—Penzance ... Pitlochry. We took him to France by Eurotunnel in May and he did a tour of the Dordogne.
Lester (*putting down the bag*) He'll be glad of the rest, then.
Janice Stool over here, please, Rosemary.

Rosemary brings the stool and puts it down a little distance off the rug and L *of the chairs*

And try to look as if you're enjoying yourself. It may be a serious occasion, but there's always room for restrained enjoyment.

Rosemary grunts, moves to extreme DL *and plonks herself down on the hump close to Elsie*

Elsie Careful! (*To Harry*) She's a weight, this one. (*To Rosemary*) Move over.

Cold Salmon

Rosemary hears this. She is surprised and worried by a voice which seems to come from nowhere, and looks about her

Rosemary What?
Pearson Are we going to have the picnic first or the ceremony?
Liz What ceremony?
Harry (*to Elsie*) She can hear you.
Elsie I don't think so. Nobody ever does. (*To Rosemary*) Can you?

No response this time. Elsie shakes her head

No.
Pearson Well, we have to scatter the ashes.
Lester That won't take long. Might as well do it at once and get it over.
Harry (*to Elsie*) Touch her.
Pearson It's a bit more than scattering, as a matter of fact. I mean ... up here, close to the sea, there's bound to be a wind. You'd get blowback. Janice wrote to the vicar in the local village.
Janice St Marion le Vaux. It's an extended parish. They have jurisdiction.
Pearson He's had a little hole dug just by the headstone. He offered to conduct a service of dedication, as a matter of fact, but Dad being a Mason I thought better not.
Harry (*to Elsie*) Go on! Touch her.

Elsie does so. She and Harry watch. No response

Janice We remove the loose earth—I've brought a trowel—pour your father in reverently——
Harry (*to Elsie*) Again! Touch her again.
Liz *Pour* him in?
Pearson The ashes. We pour the ashes in.
Janice —then replace the earth and pack it firm. After which...

Elsie puts out a hand slowly, watched by Harry, and touches Rosemary again. Rosemary shivers and gives a small cry

Harry She felt that.
Janice (*to Rosemary*) What's the matter, darling? Someone walking over your grave?
Elsie It's most unusual.
Liz (*to Janice*) After which?
Pearson After which, it was thought, one of us might make a short ... give a ... some kind of a ... few words sort of thing. Saying goodbye, Father, Godspeed, something of that nature.
Liz Who thought that, I wonder?
Lester Not me.
Janice I did.
Lester And who'll be saying the few words?
Janice Pearson. As Head of the Family.
Lester As what?
Pearson As the eldest son. Janice thought...
Liz I'll say my own goodbyes, thank you. But make a speech if you want.
Janice (*to Rosemary*) Come over here, darling. You don't look at all comfortable out on your own.

Rosemary gets up, moves over to the stool, and sits on it

Pearson I'll just... (*To Janice*) By the headstone, the vicar said?
Janice Wrote. It was in his letter. A small excavation, six by eight inches, at the left side of the headstone, professionally prepared.
Liz You mean it needed a specialist? He looked in the Yellow Pages under Small Excavations—Funereal?
Janice There's bound to be some person maintains the churchyard. He'll have done it. (*She takes the trowel out of her handbag and gives it to Pearson*) Here's the trowel.
Pearson Right. (*He goes to the place at the left of the headstone where the hole has been cut in the Gro-bag*)

Lester shields him from view when he pushes back a corner of the plastic grass to get at the slit. Pearson contines speaking through the action

Cold Salmon

A small hole ... six by eight inches—that would be eight inches deep of course. Ah! this must be it. If I could just have the urn, please, Lester. We'll dump the earth on the empty bag. *(He kneels to dig, facing downstage)*

Lester gives him the urn and remains with him, watching over his shoulder and therefore also facing downstage. Liz and Janice come up to the other side of the grave to watch. Rosemary remains where she is. During this action, Harry speaks to Elsie

Harry You spoke and she heard you.
Elsie Not the second time.
Harry You touched her and she felt it.
Elsie Not the first time.
Harry Right! Must be intermittent. An intermittent fault. But you did get through.
Elsie If you like.
Harry I've heard of it—read about it long ago—in *Titbits*, I think, or *John Bull's Weekly*, and there was a programme on the radio. It's always unhappy teenage girls have the sensitivity. Receptors, like, to the astral plane. Usually poltergeists get hold of them and they throw the furniture about.
Elsie I don't see the point in that. It'd make trouble.
Harry That *is* the point. For a poltergeist. But if *we* can communicate...
Elsie How do you know she's unhappy?
Harry Look at her mum and dad. Would *you* be happy?

Rosemary yawns. Pearson is having difficulty getting the top of the urn off—and in fact it won't come off

Pearson I think the bloody thing's welded on.
Janice Reverence, Pearson, reverence!
Pearson We can't pour the ashes in, if the top won't come off the urn. I don't know how people manage. "Scattering the ashes"! There's a lot of talk about it but you never see anyone actually doing it.

Lester We'll just have to bury the urn.

Elsie There was this Madame Jacuzzi or some such used to hold Psychic Suppers in Chorley. Twenty-five pound for a glass of red wine, a bridge roll and a chat with the departed. I hung around for a bit on the off chance, but nobody asked to speak to me.

Harry See anyone you knew? Among the departed?

Elsie No way! It was a couple of Red Indians did most of the talking.

During the following exchanges, Pearson puts the urn into the hole and covers it with earth as best he can

Pearson There's going to be a lot of earth left over: we can't pack it all flat. The urn takes up more room than ashes.

Janice Do the best you can and push the spare earth up by the headstone.

Angie and Beth enter from the church

Angie assumes that the grave is being vandalised and becomes indignant

Angie What do you think you're doing?

Pearson Please don't be alarmed. There's a perfectly simple explanation.

Angie Vandalism! Desecration of graves! I've heard of people like you. Black magic and such! Well, you can't do that here. (*To Liz*) You said it was a picnic.

Lester Black magic first. Picnic after.

Janice (*patiently*) We are burying the ashes of my husband's father in the family tomb. We have the vicar's permission.

Angie What family? You're not local.

Janice The *family* is local. (*To Pearson*) Pearson!

Pearson My great-great-grandfather was the rector here in the days when the village was thriving—late nineteenth century sort of thing. He had a lot of children—people did in those days—and they went their different ways, but many came back to be buried. And there are brass tablets in the church.

Cold Salmon

Angie What does that prove? I've no time to read tablets.
Lester Proves they had the money to buy the advertising space. Solid citizens worthy of respect.
Angie There's nobody lives here now. Three mobile homes and an organic farmer halfway to bankruptcy. (*She looks critically at the gravestone*) There's nothing to say it's a family grave.
Liz You have to know what you're looking for.
Janice Of course, the inscriptions are rather difficult to read now, but my father-in-law's family are all here—most of them. A canon of Ripon cathedral... a Knight Commander... Admirals...
Lester Lots of those.
Janice A Chief Commissioner of the Bengal Police.
Lester You can't blame Dad for wanting to be in such distinguished company. He was a bit of a crawler all his life.
Janice Lester!
Angie (*in two minds*) Well ... if you say so. I may have jumped to a conclusion. If you've a letter... It takes all sorts these days. (*To Beth*) We'll wait here quietly, Mother. They're burying someone's ashes: they've got permission. (*Loudly*) Burying ashes!
Beth Very nice.
Liz Should we begin?

Pearson has buried the urn. He taps the earth at the top with the heel of his hand, and stands up, preparing himself

Lester Want me to trample it a bit?
Pearson That won't be necessary.
Janice (*to Angie*) You and your mother are quite welcome to listen. There's nothing private and the presence of a congregation will add to the occasion.

Pearson takes a folded piece of stiff paper from an inside pocket, glances at it, coughs and begins. The paper contains the notes for his speech: he won't need to look at it often

Pearson Well, Dad, here we all are, your loving family gathered together from widely dispersed areas to wish you a fond farewell

and lasting peace. Mother sends her apologies. You wouldn't expect her to be here; you know how she feels about anything to do with death. You've had one excellent send-off already at the cremation—mother wasn't there either, of course—and the floral tributes were much admired, but I think we all felt that it was rather an impersonal affair. The clergyman in charge had never met you, knew nothing about you, and what he had to say about the Life Hereafter kind of thing, although no doubt comforting to the bereaved, did sound as if he'd said it all before and fell some way short of the mark. But Janice and I remembered how often you'd spoken about the family grave of your ancestors in the little country churchyard high on the cliffs above the sea. And we put our heads together, did a bit of a recce, took some photographs, consulted with Liz and Lester and decided to give you your wish, once we could be reasonably sure of fine weather. So now you have your wish, Father. You rest among the worthy, and you are worthy of that rest. You were the younger son of a younger son. You had to make your own way in the world without support and you did. You provided for your family. You earned respect. Now you have come home. Fare well. We shall always remember you.
(*He puts his notes away and lowers his head reverently*)

Harry What a wanker!

Janice begins to applaud, looking sideways at Rosemary to ensure that she joins in, which she does. Angie applauds, then Liz and finally Lester. The sporadic applause dies away

Beth Very nice.
Pearson Liz?
Liz 'Bye, Dad. Sleep well. (*To Pearson*) That's it.
Pearson Lester?
Lester You want me to talk to Dad?
Pearson A word. To make it unanimous.
Lester A speech! It's not my line. However... (*He addresses the grave*) What Pearson was saying wasn't to you, Dad, or for you; it was to us and for himself—to make himself feel better about how much he disliked you, you selfish old sod.

Cold Salmon

Janice looks sideways at Angie, worried at her hearing this. Angie responds with what she takes to be a reassuring smile

Liz Lester, please! It's not the time.
Lester It is the time. If he can hear me, Dad knows bloody well what *I* might say. I don't have to make a speech. Excuse me! (*He leaves the group and goes to extreme* DR *to stare out at the sea. He is blinking to keep back the tears*)
Liz (*quietly to Pearson*) I'll go. (*She goes to join Lester* DR)
Angie (*to Janice*) Thank you so much. That was most interesting. Mother would have appreciated it more but she's rather deaf. (*Loudly*) I was telling this lady you'd have appreciated the gentleman's speech.
Beth Very nice.
Angie We come here quite regular to my own dad's grave. Mother likes to sit. We shan't disturb you. (*She wheels Beth away to the other grave*)
Janice (*to Pearson*) We might as well unpack the picnic since we've brought it.

Helped by Pearson, Janice begins to unpack cutlery, crockery, plastic tumblers, paper napkins, Tupperware containers of food, corkscrew and bottles. Rosemary does not help her mother with the picnic, but stares intently at the two by the edge of the cliff. Liz and Lester speak quietly. No histrionics from Lester. There will be bitterness but it's all factual

Liz Don't go too close to the edge.
Lester Don't worry. Something usually holds me back.
Liz (*gazing at the view*) Two sailing boats ... a steamer there in the distance ... a lot of haze... And a fat man swimming close to shore.
Lester You can't know he's fat.
Liz Feminine intuition.
Lester "Made his own way"—an office manager pushed into taking voluntary redundancy at fifty-seven. Sat in the front room

for ten years, reading detective stories from the Public Library and eating his heart out, then he had a series of strokes and died of the last. Now there he lies where we put him with the canon of Ripon and all those admirals.

Liz It's what he wanted. Pearson says.

Lester He wanted to be part of something.

Liz Right...! That's not hard to understand. I think he may have been rather a joke in the Masons. I don't think he got to wear any of the more upmarket aprons.

Lester I tried to tell him, you know. About me being—how did I put it—"more attracted to men". It wouldn't have been any good trying to tell Mum; she has her own defences against the truth. "Attracted to men"! No specifics: I didn't go into detail—the cottaging or any of the other squalid ways two strangers can meet for sex in the dark.

Liz And?

Lester He was frightened. I watched the fear growing in his eyes and the sweat run down the side of his neck into his collar, and I gave up—made my excuses and left.

Liz Yes... He *was* frightened. Most of the time. One had to remember that and try to forgive.

He turns his head sharply to look at her

Lester Do you mean what I think you mean?

Liz Yes... It wasn't such a big deal. It only happened once when I was fourteen and crowding my tits into tight sweaters to make them look bigger. It didn't add up to anything. It happens to other daughters with other fathers. It happens a lot.

Lester I wanted to love him. I wanted him to love me.

She touches his arm

Liz Come back to the picnic as soon as you can. (*She returns to the others*)

Janice's contribution to the picnic has now been spread out

Cold Salmon

Janice This is the kind of occasion when Tupperware comes into its own.

Liz opens her shoulder bag and adds its contents to the spread, putting the bag down wherever it is least in the way. Her sandwiches are in plastic containers, bought from a supermarket

Liz Ham. Tuna and mayo. Cheese and pickle. I picked them up at the Superstore on my way out of Northampton. So there's also cheesecake—blackcurrant and raspberry ripple. The coffee's instant, but I did boil the kettle myself.
Janice How thoughtful! And we have brought... (*She indicates the items*) Cold poached salmon and a new potato salad with my own home-made mayonnaise. Thinly sliced cucumber in balsamic vinegar. Lettuce, hard-boiled eggs, cherry tomatoes and some dear little individual quiches of broccoli and courgette. Figs, peaches, grapes and a selection of cheeses with *focaccia* and a couple of bottles of Marks and Spencer's Special Recommendation chilled Chablis. I hope it'll be enough.
Liz More than enough, I'd say.

Lester rejoins the party

Lester Then why don't we ask that lady and her mother to join us? After all, they had to listen to the speeches.

Janice is appalled. We see the instant reaction on her face, then the quick turn of her head to Pearson and back to Lester. She mouths the words, "Not so loud"

Sorry?
Janice (*whispering*) Not ... so ... loud. You'll embarrass them.

Lester does not lower his voice. The object of the exercise is to embarrass someone and that someone is Janice

Lester Why should it embarrass someone to be asked to share a picnic?

Pearson (*quiet but compelling*) Never does to rush in.
Liz I think it's rather a good idea. As Lester says, it's not as if they were strangers: they've already heard most of the family history.

Janice looks at Pearson again. He hesitates, dithers, then...

Pearson Oh, very well, very well. (*He raises his voice to address Angie*) We were wondering whether you and your mother would care to join us.
Angie (*delighted*) Oh, we couldn't really; it's too much. (*She is already pushing Beth back to rejoin the group*) Perhaps just a bite for good fellowship. (*To Beth*) Invited to a picnic.
Beth Very nice.
Janice I'll just prepare a plate for your mother. (*She starts to put food on a plate*) Potato salad? A little quiche? Cherry tomatoes?
Angie Not too much, thank you. Mother has no more appetite than a bird.
Janice Just one cherry tomato, then.
Lester I've known birds that could pig it a bit. You've only to watch pigeons attacking the kitchen spillage from a five-star hotel.
Janice A little cold salmon?
Angie I'm afraid Mother isn't allowed cold salmon. Not with her hiatus hernia. There might be bones. She could choke.
Lester (*proffering one of Liz's sandwiches*) Tuna and mayonnaise— she could manage that. Tesco's finest: it'd go down a treat. (*He holds the sandwich towards Beth*)

Beth puts a hand out towards it. Angie interposes her own hand, takes the sandwich and puts it in her bag

Angie Best not too much at a time. It overfaces her. I'll keep it for later.
Beth (*wanting it now*) Very nice.
Janice No cold salmon.
Harry There's an idea stirring inside me. Just a germ but it'll grow. I can feel it stretching its muscles.

Janice And for you, Mrs ... er...
Angie Outhwaite. Mother's Mrs Farnham. You can see the name on the gravestone. Dad died in nineteen seventy, but she comes up every month if the weather allows.
Harry (*to Elsie*) Somewhere inside that dessicated, deaf and underfed old woman is my wife, Beth, and I mean to reach her.
Elsie We can't reach them. They can't hear us, they can't feel us, we can stand in their way with our arms out and they'll walk straight through.
Harry The girl hears. The girl feels.
Angie I would like a little salmon, please. But not the cucumber which disagrees.
Rosemary Can I have some wine?
Pearson I'll open a bottle and we'll all have some. (*To Angie*) Unless your mother...?
Angie No wine for Mother, thank you.
Beth (*dolefully*) Very nice.

As Pearson opens the bottle, a loud cry comes from Dad, concealed behind the large gravestone

Dad (*angrily*) There's nobody here.

Dad emerges from behind the family gravestone. He is wearing full morning dress—which would be grey, of course—with a grey top hat

The picnic party cannot hear or see him: they take no notice of him at all. Instead, Janice continues to fill and pass plates, Pearson to fill and pass glasses. The picnic continues throughout the following dialogue between the three dead characters, but we do not hear what is said by the living unless indicated. We should be conscious that the picnic is going on, but it should not distract us from the other action

There's nobody here at all.

Harry There's us.

Dad Three—no, I tell a lie. Four, maybe five, generations of my family, as good as any in the land, and not one of them here to welcome a new arrival.

Harry They'll have buggered off. Couldn't be bothered to wait around. Better things to do, especially the canon of Ripon; he'd have his own welcome Up Top in Abraham's bosom. Not everybody waits. Most don't.

Dad You're waiting.

Harry Nothing else to do, and anyway I'm the waiting type. (*He points at Elsie*) She's waiting, but she doesn't really know what for.

Elsie Mint Imperials.

Angie (*to Janice*) It's not a home as such: we'd never put Mother in a home. It's what they call secure residential accommodation, you might say, with her own room, meals on wheels, and there's a lady comes in one morning a week to give her a bath.

Janice I know exactly what you mean. Independence is so important at your mother's age.

Liz Yes, it is. At any age.

Janice And having a few of one's own treasured keepsakes within easy reach. Pearson and I realize that even we may have to move to a retirement bungalow in the fullness of years when our own house has grown too big for us, but there are two *cloisonné* Japanese vases which will travel with us wherever we go.

Harry You're dressed up a bit, aren't you?

Dad Gordon Bennett, the funeral director—he's a fellow Mason, known him all my life—he says if you're going to meet your Maker you might as well dress up for it and show respect. But it *is* all show mostly—fastens with Velcro at the back, and Gordon's men slip it off you to use again on someone else before you go into the furnace.

Harry You kept yours.

Dad That was Janice. When it comes to value for money, she's a stickler.

Janice I'm a stickler for value for money. You pay for what you get.

Cold Salmon

(*To Rosemary*) Have one of your auntie's sandwiches, Rosemary; you've taken nothing. We don't want you anorexic.
Dad You'd think there'd be somebody to show me the ropes. What am I expected to do? Where am I to go?
Harry It's the kind of thing your daughter-in-law might know but they seem a bit preoccupied at the moment.
Janice I brought some extra mayonnaise in a jar.
Lester Is there any more wine?
Elsie And anyway you can't get through to them.
Dad I've always done what's expected of me. Willingly. Cheerfully. But there has to be someone to tell me what it is.
Harry You want us to help you? Give you your marching orders, like?
Dad Would you?
Harry Well, I don't know: it's a lot to ask. We're no kin to you, this lady and me, not even your kind: you're a cut above us. We couldn't muster an admiral between us, even pooling our resources.
Dad Janice exaggerates. There was only one admiral and it was in wartime.
Harry You complain about nobody waiting to look out for you. (*He indicates Elsie*) She doesn't know where her own family's gone. They popped her into an unmarked grave and left without paying the sexton. Could you rely on our advice?
Dad I'd have to. There's no alternative.
Harry We'll think about it. There might be something you could do for me first. Quid pro quo, in a manner of speaking.
Dad Quid pro quo. Right. What is it?
Elsie If you're going into Latin on a regular basis, I shan't stay. I've been a strict Methodist all me life.
Harry (*to Dad; indicating Rosemary*) Take a look at the girl. Do you know who she is?

Rosemary is pushing food around her plate. Janice speaks patiently to her

Janice Don't play with your food, Rosemary.

Rosemary Haven't you got a quiche without marrow in it?
Dad It's my granddaughter Rosemary, isn't it? Pearson's daughter: they only have the one. I've not seen much of her since I retired, and what I have seen didn't impress me.
Harry It's our belief she has a deep inner life.
Dad (*looking at her; surprised*) Do you think so?
Harry Well worth the plumbing. (*He indicates to Elsie that she should back him up*)
Elsie More than meets the eye.
Harry There's a psychic sensitivity.
Dad Is there?
Harry We've already put out feelers and provoked a response. I propose to communicate. The cold salmon is the key. If the three of us link hands and concentrate our psychic forces, I think we might do it.
Elsie I tell you now, you have to have Indians. Big feathered hats and loaded with wampum. They've the experience.
Dad Where would we find them?
Elsie Chorley mainly. And Bamber Bridge.
Harry (*commanding*) We do not ... need ... Red Indians. It's a free country. Britannia rules the waves. Your hands, please. And concentrate on the girl.

They link hands. Meanwhile Liz uses a paper napkin to remove a bone from a piece of salmon in her mouth

Liz This salmon's delicious, but I have to confess Mrs Outhwaite's quite right: there are bones. (*To Angie*) Wouldn't do for your mother.
Harry Yes, it would. With any luck, it will. (*To the other two*) Come along.

They move into position behind Rosemary's chair, with Harry in the middle

Janice A little more, somebody. I hate having to take food home. Mrs Outhwaite?

Cold Salmon

Angie I couldn't.
Janice Lester?

He puts his hands up to indicate polite refusal

> Liz, just the weeniest piece.

Liz Not even the weeniest. I shall move gracefully on to figs. (*She looks at the untouched cheesecake on the rug*) I shouldn't have bought that cheesecake. I knew at the time it was conspicuous waste, but I was trying to keep my end up, I suppose. Nobody's eaten any, and quite right with such Lucullan alternatives.
Elsie What's Lucullan?
Harry More Latin, I think.
Rosemary I'd like some cheesecake.

Janice is not too happy. Again the quick look at Pearson and back again

Janice Are you sure, darling?
Rosemary You said you didn't want me anorexic.
Pearson I think it's a matter of maintaining the vitamin balance sort of thing.
Rosemary I'll have a piece, then. Raspberry ripple.

Liz puts out a hand to pass the plastic container of cheesecake. Janice gives a quick shake of the head and a grimace. Liz withdraws her hand

> I'll get it myself. (*She leaves the stool and kneels on the rug to get herself the piece of cheesecake*)

Harry Now! Concentrate the psychic forces! Cold ... salmon!
Elsie ⎫
Dad ⎭ (*together*) Cold ... salmon!

Rosemary's hand, reaching out for the cheesecake, stops, wavers for a moment, then goes to the cold salmon and grasps it. She returns to her stool and sits. She looks down at what she has in her hand

Rosemary Who gave me this...? It's cold salmon.
Janice You took it, darling. Changed your mind: I'm so glad. You're most welcome to finish up the salmon. Much better for you.
Angie Fish is good for the brain, they say.
Beth Very nice.
Pearson And full of Vitamin E, which prevents cancer. Have some cucumber with it—Vitamin A. (*To Janice*) I'm not sure about the balsamic vinegar.
Lester Running over with goodness. The elixir of life.
Rosemary I wanted cheesecake.
Harry Again!
Elsie \
Dad   } (*together*) Cold ... salmon!
Rosemary I'll put it back.
Harry All together!
Elsie \
Harry } (*together*) Cold ... salmon!
Dad
Rosemary (*to Beth*) You have it. (*She offers the cold salmon to Beth*)
Angie No! No, dear, no!
Harry Yes, dear, yes!
Angie (*loudly*) No salmon, Mother.
Janice Put it back, Rosemary. What do you think you're doing?
Beth Very nice. (*She grabs the salmon from Rosemary and stuffs it into her mouth*)

A frozen moment. Harry releases Elsie's and Dad's hands. The living characters are all watching Beth chew. It is a large mouthful and chewing takes time

Pearson I'm not sure she should have done that.
Harry (*closing his eyes*) I'm making a prayer. Hear my prayer.
Janice (*to Rosemary*) What came over you to offer the cold salmon? You knew she wasn't allowed such a thing.

Rosemary I don't know. It was just cheesecake I wanted. You confused me.
Liz Perhaps we're making a fuss about nothing. As far as I was concerned there was only that one bone.
Pearson She certainly seems to be enjoying it. (*To Angie*) Hiatus hernia, you said?

Beth swallows

> There! Down the little red lane and no harm come of it. (*To Beth*) You had us worried there for a moment, Mrs Farmer.

Angie Farnham.

Worry over, they return to the picnic

> Least said, soonest mended. We've had crises before. I've known creamed spinach give anxiety, though we've learned with experience to avoid it.

Janice Let me offer you some dolcelatte with your focaccia.

Beth makes a choking sound. They turn quickly towards her. Harry opens his eyes. Beth manages to hurl herself upwards out of the wheelchair, her hands raised in front of her, clutching at the air. She is choking and fighting for breath. Angie tries to catch and hold her

Angie Mother!

Beth pushes her out of the way, turning upstage, then falls forward. She must fall so that most of her is behind the gravestone, leaving only her feet and part of her legs in view. Angie angry, turns to confront Janice

> I knew something like this would happen. Fish of any species or temperature has not passed mother's lips for twenty years. (*She kneels by Beth's body*)

During the following dialogue, Rosemary, Liz, Janice and Lester come slowly forwards to look at the body, completely masking the exposed bits so that the ASM, identically dressed, can take Beth's place; while Pearson moves upstage to look at the body from the other side of the gravestone

 Mother...! Mother...! Say something. Are you hurt? You can tell me.
Pearson There's a Manual of First Aid in the car. *What To Do In An Emergency.* I'll bring it.
Lester We should get her up. Back to the chair.
Janice You mustn't move people. I've always heard that. (*To Liz*) Liz, you've had First Aid training at that school of yours, haven't you? Can't you do something?
Liz Stand out of the way, then.

The others, including Angie, make way for Liz. By now the substitution should have been made, and Beth is safely behind the gravestone getting out of the coat which has covered her grey dress and also getting rid of her hat; the feet and legs of the ASM have replaced hers and the audience should not know the difference. During the following, Liz comes to those feet and legs and kneels. She feels the pulse in the unseen wrist

Dad (*to Harry*) Is this what we were trying to achieve?
Harry Exactly what we were trying to achieve.
Elsie Think I'll sit for a bit, then. (*She wanders back to her place* DL)
Harry Thank you for your support.
Elsie Any time. (*She sits*)
Dad Well... as long as I don't have to take the responsibility... (*He moves back upstage out of the way*)
Harry I take the responsibility.
Liz She's dead, I'm afraid. There's nothing we can do.

Angie begins to cry. Liz holds her

 It wasn't your fault.

Janice Pearson, get the mobile from the car. We'll have to inform the authorities. Rosemary, go with your father. I'll clear up here.
Pearson (*going*) Right...! Right!

Pearson exits

Rosemary (*to Liz*) Did I do it?
Liz No.
Rosemary I never meant to.
Liz She grabbed the salmon out of your hand. Mrs Outhwaite knows that. (*To Lester*) Go with her, Lester.

Lester goes off with Rosemary, his arm round her shoulders, in the direction of the car

Beth comes from behind the gravestone. She is now in her sixties. Angie's sobs become more muted as Liz holds her. Janice continues to pack up the picnic

Beth Harry...?
Harry Over here. Waiting.

He comes to Beth, takes her hand and leads her towards L

Dad Here! Just a moment! We had a bargain.
Harry (*stopping and turning to him*) We did.
Dad Quid pro quo. You've had the quid; now it's time for the quo. What am *I* to do? You haven't told me.
Harry Wander. Find your own way. That's what we all do. (*He continues on his way with Beth*) Come on, lass. No point in hanging about. We've got places to go.

Light begins to fade R

Beth You've taken long enough to get me out of that bloody chair. Nigh on thirty years. I'll have your guts for garters.

Beth and Harry have reached L just above the hump of Elsie's unmarked grave. Light intensifies on the two of them. They are looking at each other. Harry puts out both hands towards her. She takes them and he draws her in to his body. They kiss passionately. Both are close to tears

Dad You can't leave me here with nobody.
Harry (*to Beth*) I've missed you. So much.
Beth I've missed you an' all.
Elsie I'll wait a bit longer. You never know.

Slow fade

CURTAIN

FURNITURE AND PROPERTY LIST

Further dressing may be added at the director's discretion

On stage: Large grave and large gravestone with weathered inscription
Smaller grave and stone cross on a base, with readable inscription. *On grave:* container with dead flowers
Unmarked grave

Off stage: Wheelchair containing **Beth** (**Angie**)
Plastic bag containing pot of seasonal flowers (**Beth**)
Shoulder-bag containing sandwiches in plastic containers, cheesecake, thermos with coffee (**Liz**)
Large handbag containing trowel (**Janice**)
2 cool-bags containing cutlery, crockery, plastic tumblers, paper napkins, corkscrew, 2 bottles of wine, Tupperware containers of cold salmon, potato salad, cucumber in vinegar, lettuce, hard-boiled eggs, cherry tomatoes, figs, peaches, grapes, cheeses, quiches; large car rug, 2 folding chairs, small folding stool (**Pearson**)
Plastic bag containing urn wrapped in bubblewrap (**Lester**)

Personal: **Beth**: long coat, hat
Liz: piece of card, wristwatch
Pearson: folded piece of stiff paper
Dad: grey top hat

LIGHTING PLOT

Property fittings required: nil
1 exterior. The same throughout

    To open: Late morning/early afternoon summer lighting

    Cue 1   **Harry**: "We've got places to go."   (Page 25)
               Fade lighting R

    Cue 2   **Beth** and **Harry** reach L above **Elsie**'s grave   (Page 26)
               Intensify lighting on them

    Cue 3   **Elsie**: "You never know."   (Page 26)
               Slowly fade to black-out

EFFECTS PLOT

Cue 1   **Angie**: "Hold that."   (Page 3)
           Sound of car stopping off, then car door slams

Cue 2   **Angie** wheels **Beth** away and **Liz** shrugs   (Page 4)
           Sound of car stopping off

Cue 3   **Angie** exits with **Beth**   (Page 4)
           Sound of four car doors closing

www.ingramcontent.com/pod-product-compliance
Lightning Source LLC
Chambersburg PA
CBHW070454050426
42450CB00012B/3277